ST DAVI
PC

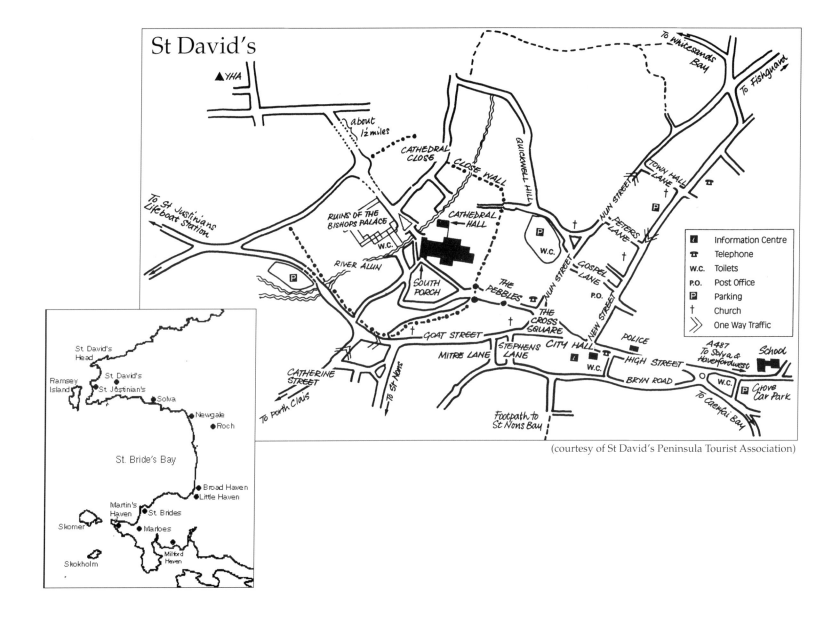

(courtesy of St David's Peninsula Tourist Association)

ST DAVID'S & ST BRIDE'S BAY

POSTCARDS OF YESTERYEAR

Brian Cripps

First impression—May 1997

ISBN 1 85902 492 0

© Brian Cripps

Printed at
Gomer Press, Llandysul, Ceredigion

ACKNOWLEDGEMENTS

I have experienced much satisfaction and joy in collecting the viewcards within this publication. I do hope that the reader will likewise enjoy this pictorial walk down memory lane and marvel at the skill of the postcard photographers whilst turning the pages of this latest volume in the Yesteryear series.

This book would not have been possible without the kind assistance of others. In particular, I acknowledge the help of Mr David Mendus of Aberdesach, Gwynedd, for providing details of his father's career, and for the loan of the two photographs of William Morris Mendus, one of which shows him using his own half-plate camera.

In addition I wish to thank Dr G. W. Middleton MBE of St David's for his co-operation and for providing valuable historical information. My thanks also to Steven and Robert Hughes of Burry Port for their continued help.

I again thank my dear wife Lorna for her unfailing patience and support. I also wish to thank Dyfed Elis-Gruffydd and the staff of Gomer Press for pointing me in the right direction when it mattered.

Brian Cripps

FOREWORD

The historic 'village' City of St David's stands in beautiful countryside and near the coastline of western Pembrokeshire. This coastline is a succession of beauty spots running down St Bride's Bay like a string of pearls.

St David's is best known for its cathedral situated in the valley floor alongside the River Alun, but it can also claim to be the smallest city in Britain, with a population of about 2,000. This tiny city is dedicated to the memory of Dewi, Wales' patron saint, with its cathedral as the focal point of worship and pilgrimage.

Synonymous with St David's is its famous R.N.L.I. Lifeboat Station on the coast at St Justinian's. The boathouse dating from 1869 commenced with its first lifeboat the *Augusta* and today houses a Tyne-class boat named *Garside.*

Within this volume of 110 postcard views I aim to show St David's and district as the area appeared to photographers from 1901 to the 1960s. The skills of local photographers such as William Morris Mendus are clearly evident and a tribute to their professionalism. Some pictures will be familiar to many readers, whilst other views have hitherto been known to but a few enthusiasts.

In 1994 the hobby of postcard collecting celebrated the centenary of picture postcards (1894-1994). I have chosen from my own collection viewcards ranging from St David's Head in the north down through St Bride's Bay to a southerly point at Marloes village. It will, I trust, be of particular interest to all those interested in social and local history.

Brian Cripps

WILLIAM MORRIS MENDUS (1899-1969)

William Morris Mendus, born in Haverfordwest, settled in St David's in 1921. He was a qualified chemist and joined his brother John Mendus who had recently acquired the chemist shop in Cross Square from Mr Albert David. In 1930 William Morris married Miss Margorie Prance of Solva and set up home in Grove Villa, St David's. Here their two children Janet and David were born.

The three Mendus brothers, Elwyn, John and William Morris, outside the family Chemist Shop in Cross Square, St David's, *c.* 1922 (courtesy of Mr David Mendus).

About 1926 William Mendus became deeply interested in photography and five years later, after acquiring the chemist shop from his brother John, he began selling picture postcards. The cards, which proved popular and sold very well, were, in fact, photographic views of St David's and district which William Morris had taken with his own half-plate camera. William Morris also developed his own photographs and subsequently sold camera roll-film produced by Kodak, Selo, Lukos and Agfa.

William Morris was a member of the St David's R.N.L.I. Lifeboat Station for 25 years and its chairman for 5 years. Photographs of the lifeboat and the boathouse soon found their way into his rapidly expanding collection of postcards, as did views of the Pembrokeshire coastline.

The earliest examples of W. M. Mendus postcards in this book date from 1931. Many of his photographs have also found their way into local publications and guide-books relating to the St David's area. Without question, William Morris Mendus has earned his place amongst the finest commercial photographers in Pembrokeshire, and those in this volume bear testimony to his skill between 1931 and 1967.

William Morris Mendus photographing St David's Cathedral with the aid of his half-plate camera, *c.* 1967 (courtesy of Mr David Mendus).

On his retirement William Morris Mendus sold the business to his daughter and son-in-law Mr D. G. Hampson.

Brian Cripps

A multiview card of the St David's area by Valentine and Sons, *c.* 1938.

A youth looks out to sea from the summit of Carn Llidi overlooking St David's Head. The card is postmarked 1953.

A Francis Frith card of Traeth Mawr, or Whitesand Bay, near St David's, *c.* 1939. Caravans were few and far between in those days.

A 1968 viewcard of Whitesand Bay by D. G. Hampson who took over the chemist shop in St David's from W. M. Mendus in 1967.

St Justinian's, Ramsey Sound and the northen tip of Ramsey Island, *c.* 1938. The photograph was taken by W. M. Mendus.

The Youth Hostel near Whitesand Bay.

The sixteenth-century ruins of St Justinian's Chapel.

St Justinian's in 1916.

This superb postcard is postmarked August 1904 and is a rare picture of the St David's lifeboat *Gem* (1885-1910). Note the cork life-jackets worn by the crew of 15.

The St David's Lifeboat Station at St Justinian's was opened in April 1869. This viewcard shows men painting the roof and walls. In the background (right) is Ramsey Island. W. M. Mendus published the viewcard in the 1940s.

This viewcard, postmarked May 1949, shows the bungalow and R.N.L.I. boathouse at St Justinian's.

The St David's lifeboat *General Farrell* (1911-36) heads into Ramsey Sound. This W.M. Mendus card is postmarked July 1938.

A grey seal pup on Ynys Dewi or Ramsey Island. The card, postmarked 1932, was published by W. M. Mendus.

The twin caves at Porth Llaudy, south-west of Ramsey Island. This atmospheric viewcard was posted at St David's Post Office in August 1916.

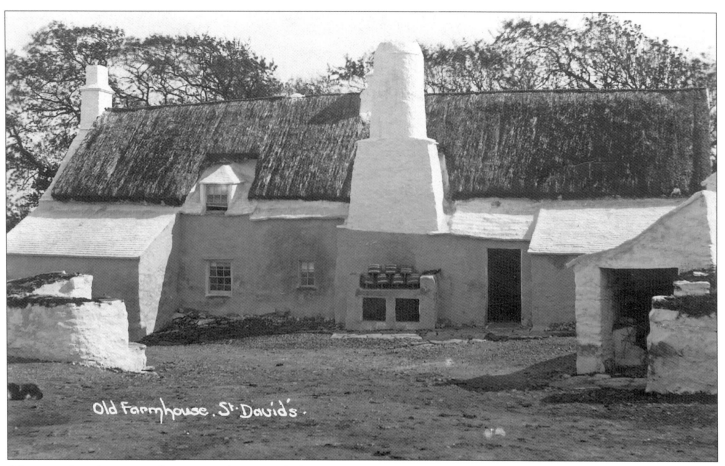

Old Farmhouse. St. David's.

Rhosson farmhouse with its round external chimney, near St Justinian's. Richard Fenton, author of *A Historical Tour through Pembrokeshire* (1810), was born at Rhosson in 1747. This W. M. Mendus card is dated *c.* 1938.

PORTHCLAIS (ST DAVIDS)

An early 1903 viewcard of Porth-clais harbour, the port which served the monastic community at St David's. From the early Middle Ages until the early twentieth century Porth-clais was a busy harbour dealing in timber, corn, malt, wool, limestone and coal.

A ladder leans against the *Bessie Clark* at low tide at Porth-clais harbour, at the mouth of the River Alun.

PORTH CLAIS, ST. DAVIDS

Copyright
S.D. 52

A ketch berthed at high tide in Porth-clais harbour. The card is by Raphael Tuck.

Porthclais, St. Davids

C.30.

High tide at Porth-clais. The photograph is by W. M. Mendus.

Probably one of the earliest picture cards posted illustrating St David's Cathedral. The card is postmarked Cardiff, 27 July 1901, and was published by Raphael Tuck.

This fine view of the cathedral is an example of the early work of W. M. Mendus. As well as being a keen local photographer, he was also a dispensing chemist in Cross Square, St David's.

St Davids - Winter.

One of several W. M. Mendus wintertime viewcards of St David's Cathedral sold as a Christmas greeting card. The card dates from the 1950s.

A superb W. M. Mendus card of a winter scene near the cathedral.

St. Davids – Winter.

A fine postcard of the St David's Cathedral choirs stalls by Francis Firth. The card is postmarked Haverfordwest, August 1901.

The choir and presbytery looking east towards the high altar. The card is dated August 1913. Recent research has shown that the oak casket, set in the west wall of Holy Trinity Chapel beyond the high altar, possibly contains the mortal remains of St. Caradog who died in 1124.

The cathedral nave, looking east, by W. M. Mendus. The card is postmarked 1951.

The Pebbles, leading to Porth-y-twr or the Tower Gateway, *c.* 1900.

CATHEDRAL APPROACH, ST. DAVID'S

D.46

The Tower Gateway and St David's Cathedral. The photograph was taken by W. M. Mendus in the 1950s.

THE TOWER GATEWAY (PORTH-Y-TWR), ST. DAVID'S

D.45

A 1950s viewcard of the Tower Gateway. The car registration is SDE 260. Does anyone recall this number?

The Bell Tower and Thirty-Nine Articles, St. David's

The thirty-nine steps, also known as the Thirty-nine Articles, leading up to the Tower Gateway, 1932. The octagonal Bell Tower dates from the thirteenth century.

The Thirty-nine Articles, Tower Gateway and part of
the city from the roof of St David's.

An aerial view of St David's Cathedral, the Bishop's Palace and Goat Street (foreground). The card is postmarked 15 June 1922.

An aerial view of the Bishop's Palace and St David's Cathedral, published by W. M. Mendus, *c.* 1946.

An aerial view of St David's Cathedral and the Bishop's Palace. Quickwell (a corruption of the welsh *cwcwll*, meaning 'cowl') Hill is in the background. The photograph was taken in 1956.

Bishop's Palace, St. David's

A fine view of the Bishop's Palace, postmarked July 1913.

The Bishop's Palace from the roof of St David's Cathedral.

An aerial view of the Alun valley, north of the cathedral close, by D. Bowen and Son, *c.* 1914. In the background are the craggy summits of Carnedd-lleithr and Carn-ffald.

This 1906 card shows ladies assembled in front of the Cross in readiness to welcome H.R.H. Duke of Edinburgh in 1882.

St. Davids, The Cross.

Two horse-drawn carts complete this 1906 view of Cross Square.

This view of the fourteenth-century cross was taken in 1914. On the wall of the building on the left are two advertising boards drawing attention to Thorleys Cakes. The summit of Carn Llidi stands in the background.

A superb photographic postcard of Cross Square by D. Bowen, taken *c.* 1915. The Captain Roach Fountain was erected in 1914.

Cross Square by the Photochrome Company Ltd. of Tunbridge Wells, *c.* 1925. Note the motor cycles with side-cars.

Cross Square and Tabernacle chapel (left) leading into Goat Street, *c*. 1932. Note the First World War field gun. The card is by John Mendus.

Arthur Squibbs, the Tenby photographer, took this view of Cross Square in 1942.

The Second World War (1939-45) Memorial Gardens, Cross Square, 1950.

The Second World War Memorial Gardens, 1950. On the right is W. M. Mendus's chemist shop.

Old Cross Hotel during the 1950s. The photograph is the work of W. M. Mendus. He would have seen this view from his chemist shop, situated opposite the hotel.

A horse-drawn brake is unloaded outside St David's Post Office, 1902. Mr Mathias, the postman, awaits receipt of the day's mail bag. The building partly obscured by the brake is the old butcher's shop.

(courtesy of Dr. G. W. Middleton)

Children stop to gaze at the 'horseless carriage' in Cross Square, 1903. The car was owned by the village doctor.

(courtesy of Dr G. W. Middleton)

Nun Street, by W. Ll. Evans of St David's.

High Street and the City Hall, 1928. The plaque by the entrance to the hall is to Captain Samuel Roach. The City Hall now houses the tourist information office and library.

The old stone-faced building on the left was the original home of Barclays Bank until the business moved into newer premises next door. This card is dated *c.* 1946.

A cavalcade of ladies marching in column down the High Street, St David's, past the building which later housed Barclays Bank during the 1920s. Was this a Mothers Union Parade? Note the old car (centre) and garage (left).

A second view of the same parade (see page 63). The banner reads Llanon Parish Carmarthenshire.

A flag bedecked Goat Street, St David's, celebrating the Royal Jubilee in May 1935. A bicycle leans against the wall of the Farmers Arms.

An aerial view of St David's by Aerofilms but sold by John Mendus, the town's chemist. The photograph was probably taken in 1929.

Cross Square, St David's by Aerofilms of Hendon, published by John Mendus, *c.* 1932.

The old car, registration plate DR 2061, stands by a rather neglected Memorial Gardens and flagpole, erected in 1912 to commemorate victims of the R.N.L.I. *Gem* disaster.

Survivors of the *Gem* lifeboat disaster. On the night of 12 October 1906 the *Gem* was wrecked on the rocks known as the Bitches in Ramsey Sound. The coxswain and two crew members perished.

The Grove Hotel. The card, postmarked April 1906, is by Fred J. Jones.

Tŵr-y-felin Hotel, St David's, during the 1930s. Tŵr-y-felin, as the name suggests, was erected as a windmill in 1804. It was converted into a hotel a century later. It is now an adventure centre.

Tŵr-y-felin Hotel, *c.* 1947.

Glan-y-Môr, Caerfai Bay Road. The card is postmarked January 1921.

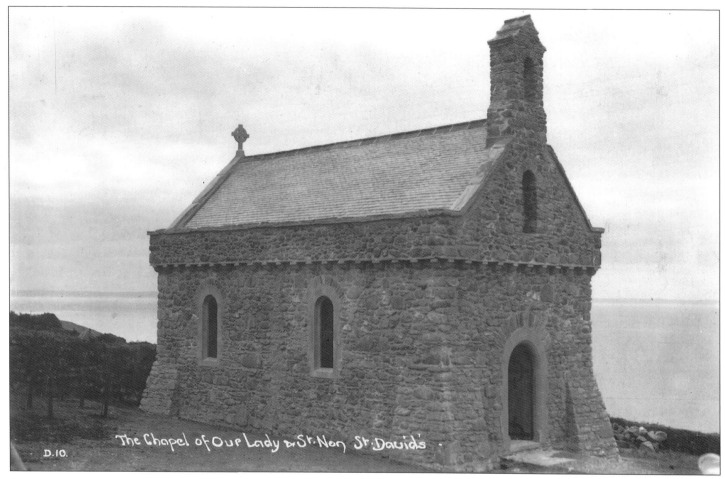

The Chapel of Our Lady & St. Non St. David's.

D.10.

St Non was the mother of St David (born *c*. 520 AD) and this renovated medieval chapel, overlooking St Non's Bay, is dedicated to her memory. This W. M. Mendus card is postmarked 1964.

Caerfai Bay was one of the sources of the beautiful purple Caerbwdy sandstone, one of the local stones used to build St David's Cathedral.

Children bathing in Caerfai Bay. One of the lads has forgotten his swimming trunks! This card was published by D. Bowen and Son in 1912.

A general view of Upper Solva.

This card was sent from Mount Pleasant, Solva, to an address in Roach, Cardiff, on 30 August 1913. The young woman carries tin cans to the communal village water tap. It was hard work in those days carrying heavy, water-filled cans.

A Francis Frith card of Upper Solva.

A rowing-boat race at the Solva Regatta, *c.* 1910, draws crowds of spectators. The bow of the ship *Dolphin* can be seen on the left.

Solva harbour by C. M. Rees. The card is postmarked 1912.

High tide at Solva harbour by C. M. Rees.

THE GRIBBIN FROM THE HARBOUR, SOLVA.

W.4528.

A Valentine card of Solva harbour and the Gribin, at the foot of which lies a row of renovated lime-kilns.

Solva harbour entrance, by the photographer C. M. Rees.

Middle Mill, a mile up-valley of Solva harbour, *c.* 1906. The woollen mill still produces woollen carpets, tweeds, travel rugs and clothing. The card was published by C. M. Rees.

Newgale Sands, Pem.   D. B. & S. 1226.

Looking south across Newgale Sands long before it became a popular holiday location. The card is postmarked August 1906.

A David Bowen card of Newgale looking west towards Dinas-fach. The card is postmarked August 1908.

A horse-drawn brake conveys passengers over the road bridge at Newgale, *c.* 1910.

Newgale Sands Cafe (white roof) has a single petrol pump outside. Note the ladies picnicking by the bridge. The card is postmarked August 1928.

An incoming tide at Newgale beach, *c.* 1912.

The storm beach at Newgale, *c.* 1926. Note the row of superb motor cars parked alongside the road.

Tents, caravans and a converted bus camped on the marshy land behind the storm beach, Newgale, *c.* 1948.

Castell y Garn or Roch castle, south-east of Newgale. Adam de la Roche, who lived in the twelfth century, was the first lord of Roch.

A rare postcard of the post office at Roch, which opened for postal services in 1896.

Nolton Haven, *c.* 1907. Coal from nearby coal-mines was exported from the harbour during the nineteenth and early part of the twentieth century.

Broad Haven viewed from the high cliffs at the north end of the beach.

A prominent sea stack at the northern end of Broad Haven beach.

Edwardian ladies enjoy a day on Broad Haven beach.

A superb photographic view of swingboats at Broad Haven. This card, published by Madam C. C. Higgs, is postmarked 1918.

A fine view of Broad Haven. The card is postmarked November 1904.

Looking north across Broad Haven beach. This photograph of an Edwardian beach fair was taken by Samuel J. Allen.

Holiday makers enjoy Broad Haven beach at low tide.

An Arthur Squibbs card showing holiday makers enjoying the sea front at Broad Haven, *c.* 1927.

Broad Haven beach by Arthur Squibbs. The card is postmarked 1938.

Walton West War Memorial, near Broad Haven.

Little Haven: the old pub on the right is the Swan. This Frith card is postmarked Milford Haven, June 1906.

Little Haven in the 1930s.

This photographic card was sent from Shawberry Road, Little Haven, in 1917, and published by Madame C. C. Higgs, Haverfordwest.

A fine photographic view of Little Haven, looking seawards, *c.* 1914.

Little Haven by Arthur Squibbs, *c.* 1932.

Little Haven: the card is dated *c.* 1949.

An apparently deserted Little Haven.

St Bride's mansion the nineteenth-century home of William Edwardes, Lord Kensington, and farm. The card is postmarked 1912.

ST. BRIDES, LITTLE HAVEN.

An imposing view of St Bride's mansion published by Hadfield, Milford Haven.

Marloes — Pem.

A fine view of Marloes village. The card was written at the Swan Inn, Little Haven, and postmarked July 1906.

Marloes village green, *c.* 1906.

Marloes village, *c.*1932. The clock tower was built in 1904 in memory of Lord Kensington. The card was published by Squibbs of Tenby & Pembroke Dock.

A superb photographic card of Marloes Post Office. Mum and the children pose outside for the camerman. The card was posted in Clunderwen on 17 August 1928.

A rare view of Martin's Haven by Arthur Squibbs, *c.* 1932. This sheltered cove is the embarkation point for boats visiting the islands of Skomer and Skokholm.

The name Skomer is Norse. In addition to its population of grey seals, the island is renowned for its breeding colonies of guillemots, razorbills, puffins, Manx shearwaters and kittiwakes.

Grassholm lies 10 miles off the Pembrokeshire coastline. It boasts one of the largest breeding colonies of gannets in Britain.

Pembrokeshire photographers who produced pictures illustrated in this book:

William M. Mendus	Fred J. Jones
Albert David	W. Ll. Evans
John Mendus	M. J. Owen
D. G. Hampson	C. Edwards
Arthur Squibbs	C. M. Rees
Samuel J. Allen	B. Hennassey
D. Bowen and Son	C. G. Griffiths
Henry M. Allen	Hadfield Series
J. D. H. Series	Scott
B. Green	Madam C. C. Higgs

Other publishers

Valentines, Dundee	Aerofilms
Raphael Tuck	Aero Pictorial Ltd
Francis Frith	Air-views, Manchester
Judges Ltd	Paul Bartalot
Photochrome Co.	
Lilywhites	